Finding the Rainbow

The Other Side of a Cancer Journey

by LeeAnn Tripp

DORRANCE PUBLISHING CO
EST. 1920
PITTSBURGH, PENNSYLVANIA 15238

Dorrance Publishing Co
585 Alpha Drive
Suite 103
Pittsburgh, PA 15238
Visit our website at *www.dorrancebookstore.com*

ISBN: 979-8-88925-012-8
eISBN: 979-8-88925-512-3

Finding the Rainbow

The Other Side of a Cancer Journey

Table of Contents

"I have fought a good fight,

I have finished my course,

I have kept the faith."

-2 Timothy 4:7

Dedicated to all the dreamers, rainbow chasers, dark horses and underdogs. Also, to those in my tribe – you know who you are, and there is no measure for my infinite thanks for your love and support.

Chapter 1

Introduction

After thousands of years attempting to crack the code for what Siddhartha Mukherjee masterfully titled *The Emperor of All Maladies*, medicine is mercifully catching up to control and improve quality of life for patients with cancer. Meanwhile, the formally leper-like disease has long shed its stigma. Now, oddly and in great contrast to the past, a disease once whispered has become commercialized in U.S. culture. We see this every fall when pink dominates October; from local carwashes to NFL games, it is nearly impossible to miss breast cancer's signature color branding throughout the month. Cancer ribbons, meanwhile, are donned year-long in the form of car decals, tattoos, lapel pins, and elsewhere.

When a cancer diagnosis hits home, loved ones spring into action, running off an invisible playbook of norms. They form groups, which become prayer warriors or tribes. The tribes become hashtags and labels on T-shirts and other merch. The hashtags inspire fundraising pages. The pages are shared. The shares are shared and so on.

While all these intentions are certainly well meaning—from the cancer awareness dominations to the proverbial acts of cancer spot kindness—they obscure a side to cancer we don't see. In fact, it's one that rarely, if ever, gets talked about. For the ones who "fight" and "win" their battles (we'll unpack those terms later), it's a messy, emotional turbulence for which nothing can prepare you. Just when you've absorbed the shock of a cancer diagnosis and the torture that comes with treatment, you are now poised to join the ranks of survivorship.

Most people associate this word (survivorship) with celebration and victory—balloons and confetti blasting across a stage where the winner stands front and center, crown affixed, glowing like a champion. While this may be true for some, for others, the realities of survivorship include an isolating and at times bitterly hopeless feeling that comes from remission.

Like a virtual purgatory, remission invites an uncomfortably weird space in which you (the patient) are not sick, but you're not well. The other proverbial shoe has not yet fallen. The support that rallied around you also begins to fall away. The greeting cards stop arriving. The prayer chains are over. The fundraising pages are archived, the cute hashtags no longer trend among friends, and the world moves on, seemingly no worse for the wear.

While one cannot expect this level of support to continue indefinitely, you—the cancer survivor—have been indelibly altered, both in DNA and more importantly, in strength and spirit. For me, re-entering the world post cancer was not the victorious, blasted-confetti-across-the-stage feeling. Rather, I felt stung in a moment of grief so painful and so unexpected it took me longer to heal from it than the cancer itself. I grieved for my old life. I ached for a time when I was unburdened by an elephant of worry and anxiety. I yearned for the days when I could fall asleep on my own without a cocktail of antidepressants and anxiety meds. And, of course, I missed the community of cheerleaders who had rallied around me. Like the rest of the world, they too had moved on.

If you are embarking on a cancer journey right now, or you know someone who is, you should earmark this page, close this book, and put it on the shelf for a day when you are stronger. Save your energy for what is in front of you now. This can wait. But, if dealing with seemingly unexplainable emotions after a cancer diagnosis and treatment are part of your journey, I encourage you to read on. You are not alone. I hope this book brings you some small comfort in your journey. If nothing else, I hope you find moments that bring laughter as you may recognize things we may share in our journeys. Above all, though, I hope you find yourself nodding along as I recount the steps of my story. Perhaps you'll say, "Yes, that's me" or "I get that." When and if you do, please think of me smiling and nodding right along back, whispering, "Yes, I know. And I get it too."

All my life, I've felt a nudge that I held something special; that something somehow set me apart from others. Maybe everyone believes themselves to be special in this way. For me, it's a sensation I've held since birth. I can recall a particular moment that happened when I was just a few weeks old.

My parents had brought my older brother and me to mass for what appeared to be a typical Sunday service.

The priest made his way up the aisle and to the front. As he was about to begin the service, he turned and paused peculiarly. "Ladies and gentlemen," he announced. "Before I begin today's service, I simply must take a moment to show you something." He then proceeded toward the crying room at the back of the church. "May I?" he asked one of the women sitting with the kids.

She stretched me, a newborn bundle, out to the priest. He carried me up the aisle and to the alter, then hoisted me in the air. "Is this not," he boomed, "the most beautiful thing you have ever seen?"

With that, the church erupted in applause with my parents feeling equal parts proud and shocked at the fuss over me.

I don't know if that was a spiritual premonition or a blessing over my life. Either way, I can't help but feel there was always a plan to set me apart in some way—certainly not on the path *I* would choose but a journey worth sharing, nonetheless. Like you, I've had many journeys during life—marriage, raising children, new careers, unexpected deaths, relocating back to and then again away from my hometown, etc. Like the oak seeded within the acorn, each journey brought lessons on loss, love, and life throughout. Of all the journeys in my life, though, the most significant and unexpected was undoubtedly my cancer story.

To be sure, this short memoir is not my life story, but a significant story from my life. I've been blessed with the gift of time to reflect and share the lessons learned along the way. Herein lies the purpose for this book: to share my unexpected cancer survival journey and, in doing so, to provide hope for those who feel abandoned, restore sanity to the ones who feel confused or spinning, and, if I'm really successful, offer or inspire a path to finding the rainbow after the storm.

"I have great respect for the past. If you don't know where you've come from, you don't know where you're going."

– Maya Angelou

Chapter 2

Roots

While this book is meant to tell a story from my life—not quite my life story—knowing where I've been is helpful to understanding where I am today.

My parents were high school sweethearts who graduated in the summer of '77 and married two years later. As ravenous music lovers, their list of concerts could rival that of the hardest rock and roller—Aerosmith, Pink Floyd (their favorite), the Rolling Stones, Billy Joel, Bruce Springsteen, Paul McCartney, Elton John, and Chicago were just a few of the headliners they'd seen.

My mom, voted funniest in her high school graduating class, came from a tough, poor home, and was the youngest of four.

She had a spicy Italian mother and an emotionally absent German father whom I never met. He was a stubborn, careless man. There are only a few facts I know about him to this day: 1. He was an army sergeant-turned-railroad worker, and 2. He wore his initials (WAM) on his work shirts. When asked what the initials stood for, he'd bark the lie, "Women." He was a loveless drunk and a cheater, and he died before I was born.

His wife, my grandmother, Frances, was his complete foil. She was an open book, a big-hearted lover who laughed easy, wore bright red nails, and gleefully chain-smoked her days through soap operas and game shows. She fried her meals in a cast iron pan and gave me the run of her house when I visited as a little girl. Could I jump on her couch all night with "Rich Girl" repeating, loudly, on vinyl? No problem. Okay, if I decorated her house for Christmas… in April? Sure thing. Cool if I dig up mudpies all afternoon by the front porch? Go for it. Can I walk to the store to get a candy bar? She'd hand me a blank check with a note for the store manager to cash whatever I spent and throw in a pack of Marlboro Red 100's.

Through all my wild child antics during the weekends and summers I spent with her, she only scolded me once. It happened when my brother and I were in a heated standdown outside and, on a dare, I doused him with a bucket of gasoline my uncle had left in the garage (as a reminder, this was the early eighties, a time when things like seatbelts—and carcinogens—were mere personal choices). Even then, she was gentle with her words and was back to scooping me ice cream later that night.

My father came from a home with a loving, hardworking father who ran a dairy. My dad was one of five children—born smack in the middle—and his mother (Grandma Marge) was a proper woman who wore long crystal necklaces, nylons and minded the home. The walls of her dining room were lined with collectors' plates and the house was spotted with stuffy, expensive, antique furniture. At one time, she operated an antique shop in a co-op, a place where us kids could not touch anything. She was unaffectionate toward me and favored her male grandchildren. There were hardly any snacks or treats in her cupboard, save for some Ritz crackers and peanut butter. Her meals were always baked, never fried. The only toys in her home were a cast iron truck and a set of wooden alphabet blocks—except if you count the two unopened, life-sized special edition Cabbage Patch dolls that tortured me from her bedroom. She was hoarding those to cash in on a lucrative sale someday (spoiler: the sale never happened). It was up to my brother, my cousins, and me to invent our own fun in Grandma Marge's house, which almost always resulted into mischief, like shattering an antique vase or upsetting a seasonal sideboard display. While often distant and quiet, Grandma Marge still had subtle ways of showing her love. Each Christmas, she would set up a mini tree in the dining room decorated in ornaments with each family member's name lovingly scripted by her in glitter glue. Every year, it was magical to search the tree with my brother, looking to find our treasured bulbs tucked within the tinsel and pine.

Holiday gatherings with my dad's family would carry on from the late afternoon until the early hours of the next morning, with the women playing rummy in the living room and the men shooting pool and downing Stroh's under a cloud of cigarette and cigar smoke in the basement. My cousins and I would run between the two floors, sometimes fighting but mostly laughing until we wore ourselves out and crashed on the couches upstairs.

There were many nights I remember my parents driving us home from that house in the pitch dark, exhausted from the day. At that time, we had lived in a rough town not far from both grandparents' homes. As naïve twenty-somethings with two kids, my folks were suckered into purchasing an overpriced home passed down from my father's shrewd grandfather. My mother stayed at home and did her best to add her warm touches to the otherwise shoddy, cold, small brick house.

When they first moved there, my father was in-between jobs when my mom saw an ad in the paper for a small company in town looking to hire a machinist. Although he didn't have much experience, my father was a natural laborer and a fast learner. Plus, the job was within walking distance, so sharing a car would not be as difficult for them. My father went down and put his application in for the position. After a few days passed without word from the shop, my mother called and pleaded with the owner to give my dad a chance, presenting a compelling case of his loyal, hardworking, and honest nature. My dad went on to work thirty plus years there, mainly with the same crew; a company that felt more like family, they saw each other through the loss of parents and spouses, and they bonded over holiday parties, summer picnics, and poolside barbecues. When the economic recession hit in 2008, that was the end of the line for the small machine shop where my dad cut his teeth.

My parents raised my brother and me on classic rock, tough love, hard work, and fresh air. When I was growing up, my dad was at the shop every day by five. He came home at two, put on his favorite rock station, and went to work at the latest house project—putting on a porch, installing a new kitchen, switching out an appliance, replacing an electrical unit, basically anything that required his handywork. My mom cooked dinner every day and we always sat together to enjoy her pick for the main course along with the staples of our dinners: whole wheat bread and butter with a cold glass of whole milk.

I was fortunate to grow up in an era when you headed, and stayed, outside from early morning until sunset. We had friends on all sides of the block where we lived and cycled through ways to pass the time. Street hockey, four squares, jacks, kickball, tag, release, king of the hill, red rover—if there was a game we could try, we played it. From spring to fall, we built forts in the woods from scrap wood with our dads' tools and wore down our sneaker soles. In the winter, we made extra money by selling homemade wreaths and shoveling driveways. As we got older, my brother and I earned our fun on the weekends by cleaning bathrooms and scrubbing kitchen floors on our knees. This would buy us a night at the skating rink or getting dropped off at the movies. While my folks did not pressure us to be overachievers, it was expected that we do our best and stay the hell out of trouble (or at least not get caught). The threat of my dad's leather belt kept it that way. There was an occasional (and memorable) stray, however, like the time my brother came home blasted at sixteen from a night out with friends. He tried to slither into the house without my parents noticing but my mom caught him just in time, and there was no hiding.

"You want to drink like a man?" she dared him. "Then you take it like a man."

With that, he was ushered out of the house to spend a chilly early spring night outside. He broke his way into the shed and curled up with a beach towel. He never came home drunk like that again, and I learned never to dare try.

While hard lessons from a blue-collar home taught me grit at a young age, nasty betrayals from former friends in middle school seared it. When I was twelve, my grandma Franny (the fun grandmother) passed away very suddenly from lung cancer. It was, and still to this day remains, the saddest moment in my life, leaving a void that has remained unfilled. Vulnerability from the death of my grandmother coupled with the angst of adolescence made me an easy target for my peers; I was a welcome outlet for them to beat out their own anxieties and insecurities.

I can picture myself now back then. Sitting in the bathroom stall, eating my lunch—a ham and cheese with mustard sandwich on wheat bread. I was hiding from my classmates (all of them) who mercilessly bullied me on the walk to and from school and any chance they got in between. My teachers were either negligent, lazy, or unequipped to intervene. I was reduced to hiding to catch reprieve from their harassment. When my mother noticed a change in me and first asked me about it, I was too embarrassed to admit I had become subject to daily torture. Eventually, I confessed, and it only took one phone call from my mother to the head bully's mother to stop the abuse. Like a switch, the teasing went from on to off after that call, and it never happened again.

If my mother was anything, she was fiercely protective of her kids. My most favorite example of this was a time when my mother was shopping in the grocery store where my brother worked during high school. At the time, my brother was balancing the rigor of tough courses like physics and advanced calculus at school while working two part-time jobs to save for college. From a distance, my mom watched as a cantankerous old man chewed out my brother for not carrying his preferred brand of milk that day. My brother humbly apologized and explained that he was just a "stock boy," but the man would not let up and unleashed hell's fury on him, undeservingly. When my brother was out of sight, my mom casually strolled her cart over to the old man.

"Hey there," she said to him with a smirk. "That boy you were talking to there, do you know who that is?" She was fake smiling through her gritted teeth.

"No," he said, curtly.

Her smile faded and her lips pinched together.

"My son," she growled.

His eyes widened.

"And if I ever catch you talking to him or any other kid working here like that again," she threatened, "I'll knock your goddamn head off."

It was a fitting and, quite frankly, spectacular confrontation to watch. He rushed away, embarrassed and scared at the fire in my mother's eyes and words. Watching my mother defend her family taught me how and when to protect my own, perhaps the greatest lesson any mother could provide for her daughter.

A seminal moment in my transition from middle to high school was choosing to take up the clarinet and join the marching band. Where the middle school years were spent learning the notes and fingering the keys, high school years were spent mastering the instrument. Our high school band director was a legend in the field who demanded excellence at every turn – every note, every roll of the foot, every formation and reformation of a show's choreography were drilled to perfection. In the band, our days and evenings ticked to a steady metronome that reminded us of the precision in which we were expected to perform. Twelve-hour practices were not uncommon to prepare for weekend overnight competitions. It was equal parts high pressure and exhilarating, and the dividends came in the form of truly spectacular shows, regional championships, medals, trophies and welcome home parades in our honor. The band was serious business at my school, and it instilled a fierce discipline that has been carried over into all my endeavors since.

Still, there was another calling during that time that pulled me from the band world into a new terrain of unexpected success. My junior year, I became a standout in my public speaking course. While most students were understandably terrified by the thought of speaking in front of their peers, I relished the opportunity. Standing behind the podium, clutching each side of its boxy frame, I stepped into a role of commanding attention and felt – perhaps for the first time in my life – empowered through the spoken word. My speech teacher immediately signed me up for the debate team, and my meek 100-pound, five-foot frame went up against other high schoolers (mostly arrogant seniors from a nearby all-boys prep school) to debate either side of a contentious subject. Abortion, death penalty, media violence, and DNA testing are some of the hot topics that I recall. At the debate competitions, I wouldn't know which side of the argument I'd have to defend until a few minutes before I was called into the room to debate a stranger in front of a panel of judges. Nevertheless, I was always ready. And, I was a killer. I would present my most compelling case, emphasizing and articulating certain phrases as though I were on the evening news delivering late-breaking headlines. Then, I would sit and listen to the other side present while I feverishly ticked off notes to unpack and dismantle every point with a cunning counterpoint. My cross-examinations were punishing, and I often left the other student stammering and spinning in a circle of confusion caused by my ruthless and, admittedly, leading line of questioning. I never made eye contact with my opponent until the round culminated with a half-friendly clammy handshake. When it was over, I would race to the leaderboard (usually posted in some unassuming hallway of the school) to see if I advanced to the next round. Almost certainly I would, and then I'd fist pump myself before skipping off to the next round of unleashing verbal carnage on another unsuspecting opponent. I recall an excellent piece of advice one of my debate coaches offered when I was competing at the national level. We were moments away from me being called to the stage.

"Have you eaten lunch yet?" he asked me at the last minute.

"No, not yet" I muttered, as I clutched my portfolio and nervously rocked back and forth, head down like I was preparing to square up in a boxing match.

"Then you're hungry," he presumed aloud while smiling. "Good."

The advice? Stay hungry in competition. Whether I was heading into a job interview, presentation, tense meeting or employee evaluation, from that moment on, I always remembered to arrive hungry (literally). It gives you an edge and a sense of urgency that presents as confidence. That advice, perhaps more than any other, has never failed to deliver. To this day, my mother still questions why I did not go into practicing law, since I surely had a knack for public speaking and perhaps argumentative persuasion. While I went on to another professional path, the confidence and skills learned at the podium, like the disciplined pursuit of excellence picked up from band, were also carryovers well beyond my teenage years.

High school proved to be a much smoother ride for me than middle school; I found my tribe and was hitting my stride by the time senior year rolled around. When my friends started driving, weekend nights were spent cruising and hitting up parties, downing Zimas with Jolly Ranchers and puffing Camel Lights. We were reckless and carefree, untethered by careers or smartphones, riding the wave of blissful youth. I had a part-time waitressing gig at a nearby family-run Greek restaurant and was a hit with the regulars who tipped me well and requested seating in my section. While it only lasted a few years, this job was my big break in the sense it gave me confidence and taught me how to succeed working in any service industry. Looking back on that experience, I realize now that 10% of my job was just getting the order right; the other 90% was connecting with the customer, delighting them with pleasant conversation and exceptional care. I refilled drinks before they asked; I always brought extra napkins; and I made personal connections on any level that mattered—if they wore a sports jersey, they got a fist pump; if they looked dressed up, I complemented their outfits; if they seemed standoffish, I stuck to talk about the weather. Building relationships through communication. That was my true sweet spot, and I relished the opportunity. This realization—that finding a way to nurture connections with others is *the* lifeblood of any success, personal or professional—has carried me from high school to present day, no matter how challenging or daunting the path would seem. Truth is, we all long for connection— but it's not the kind we make today over a Wi-Fi spot. It's more about our shared desire to be seen, heard and valued – on any level. Connection, I believe, is what provides hope and reminds us that, yes, we matter, and we are not alone on this journey. Whether sparked by offering an unexpected compliment to a stranger or exploring safe topics (food, music, and sports often work wonderfully) to uncover a shared interest with a coworker, I'm always looking for ways to connect with others. Of course, this is not a guaranteed way to make new friends or soften relationships in or out of the home; for some, building connection through communication is like getting blood from a stone. More often, though, I find that others are open to receiving the invitation to connect. Before you talk business, before you make a transaction, before you pass a stranger, try taking a moment to slow down and connect. You may be surprised by how it goes on to change your day and, when practiced consistently over time, how it could even go on to change your life and those around you.

Despite ending my high school career on a relatively high note, when I started college, I felt sorely out of place and terrified I would fail; so much so, that I remember seeking out a tutor for an intimidating writing class. I showed up with a draft of my first writing assignment and the tutor pointed out a few recommendations, but not many. They stepped out and a supervisor for the tutoring center approached me and asked if they could look at my paper. A few minutes later, he asked if he could Xerox the paper. I said, "Sure." The following week, my professor pulled me aside to complement me on my paper and say the tutoring center contacted her because they thought I might be plagiarizing. My paper was not just good, it was *too* good. I went back to the center to assure them I was no cheater and that every word had, in fact, come from my brain to the keyboard. They ended up hiring me and I went on to become their most popular writing tutor, with a line of students out the door weekly for a chance to have me look at their paper and provide feedback. The center encouraged me to continue my education after my bachelor's degree, hinting at a possible future as an English professor, and so began my journey to an advanced degree.

In graduate school, I had another bout of imposter syndrome. I couldn't believe I had earned a graduate teaching assistantship, which meant I wasn't paying a cent for my education. Rather, the university would pay *me* to teach undergraduate writing courses. All my peers seemed funnier, smarter, wittier, and more studied than me. "I don't belong here," was my initial reaction. A little older and a little wiser, though, I learned to brush off my self-doubt and settled into being myself while bending the coursework to my strengths. I connected with professors by showing interest in their research. I used humor to provide levity during serious, heavy academic discussions. At night, I clanked frothy beers in frosted mugs with my fellow grad students to let off steam. I also published two essays and an article while balancing two part-time jobs, full-time coursework, and teaching two sections of writing courses. When I finished my master's degree, I broke precedent and became the first master's student to be named the Undergraduate Teaching Assistant of Year (an award previously given exclusively to PhD students), ending my run in higher education on a satisfying note.

While I was encouraged to pursue a PhD in English, I yearned for a career and was tired of living penny to penny; plus, the academics were too stuffy and self-absorbed for my taste. I instead went on the job market and worked my way from a marketing writer to a marketing manager and then director of brand and channel marketing strategy.

Before I started a career, though, I decided to start a family.

I met my husband at a party about a month after I started graduate school. I was charmed by his humor, watching as everyone laughed while he held court telling stories about his home. After that first night meeting him, I was hooked. I went out of my way to run into him and eventually attended a party, knowing he would be there. It was my chance, I thought, to flirt my way into something more. It worked, and so began a whirlwind romance with our engagement following just eight months later. I remember how easy and mature our relationship felt at the time. He was laid back and gentle, and I loved how he showered me with affection and attention. We vibed on everything from politics to food and music. When it came time to meet his family, I fell in love with them just as easily and swiftly as I did with my husband. Brought up in a different but similar blue-collar town, his parents were hardworking, warm, easy conversationalists and his siblings were reflections of the greatest qualities I saw in my husband—funny, honest, and loyal. Like my husband, they won my heart too.

As our relationship grew more serious, my husband and I of course had a few spats but resolved them easily with open communication and grace. This pattern of mostly vibing, occasionally spatting, and then quickly forgiving continued for the next twenty years, spanning four homes, three dogs, two cats, and two kids later.

When I think about my roots, I mainly return to my grandparents' house, the one where my father's family hosted parties and holidays. I see our family's parked cars nearly wrapping the block, each one packed with giddy kids and a mound of gifts, a plated dessert, or a Tupperware-encased side dish. I also think about that house today and how it was abandoned, then demolished, after the deaths of my grandparents (when I was eight, my grandfather had a heart attack while changing a tire in the snow; my grandma Marge went on to live thirty-plus years later and died of old age in a nursing home). The house that once breathed heavy with spirited generations gathered under its roof is now an empty grass lot. For years, I dreamt about that house and having a final visit before it would come tumbling down. But chasing the past, I've learned, is a wasted pursuit. The tug of memory, the pull of nostalgia, the longing for yesterday–it can all be so haunting. And yet the power of all that yearning cannot rebuild what once stood; not even a nail can be summoned. That's the painful blessing time yields: what was once is no longer. We are not the same people today we were yesterday. Even the greatest houses built with care can fold before you have a chance to appreciate the structure it provided in your life. The sooner we learn to actually live by this reality and be open to the constant flow of change and evolution in our lives, the easier it becomes to grow from—not be tied down—by our roots. I believe it is *only* with this growth that you can ascend to the next great destination your life is calling, no matter how difficult the journey.

If you have not done so recently, I encourage you to search your memories and unearth the roots of your past, especially the ones that may have splintered over time. Whether examining a broken relationship or a career misstep, chartering the twists and turns of your roots can be richly rewarding in developing a better sense of self. This ultimately helps to stabilize and adjust your footing as you navigate any turbulence that unsettles your present reality.

Unearthing your roots

Honoring your past is critical to navigating the present and stabilizing for an unknown future. To do this, here are a few prompts:

1. Picture the house where you spent most of your time as a child. What do you hear, feel and see? Jot down memories and consider how they shaped your path.

2. Who would be on your "Mount Rushmore" of most favorite people in your life and why? Think of how they inspired or encouraged you through any obstacle and carved your life story.

3. Was there a time you felt unsure of yourself or like an imposter? How did you overcome that feeling? Write down what did or did not work for shifting you from uncomfortable to confident. These same strategies may help you during uncertain times.

"Perhaps this is the moment for which you have been created."

- Esther 4:14

Chapter 3
December 26, 2014

In 2014, two things happened that changed my life. On October 27, I welcomed a beautiful baby boy, my second child and only son, into the world—Jameson Lee Tripp.

Like my pregnancy with my first child, I had an uneventful and, in fact, rather enjoyable pregnancy. Sure, I had the usual queasiness and fatigue in the beginning, but as my tummy swelled, along with my heart, I relished the journey. I marveled at the joy it brought out in strangers and the tender, gentle manner I was treated. Pregnancy was an excuse to baby myself. I had permission to nap and indulge as I'd like after spending the better part of my life on diet and exercise. I relished in the elastic waist pants and wide bottomed tops that tied behind my back. The world seemed to show me more kindness and grace than it had all my life, especially as the bump grew bigger and my condition became more obvious. Strangers would ask me how I was feeling, what was I having, was it my first, and so on. Blessed with the gift of gab, I was more than happy to indulge them in conversation.

Around the thirty eighth week of my first pregnancy, the doctor found I was already two whole centimeters dilated. With that news, I put myself on bedrest expecting to labor at any moment. I started my FMLA leave early and even stopped driving. "The baby is coming," I'd say dramatically, as I'd lie on the bed or couch and practice my breathing exercises.

Two weeks later, and still no baby (or increased dilation for that matter), I began an intense regimen of walking, Indian food, and pineapple. Sure enough, at around eleven p.m. on September 6 (the night before my birthday), my water broke. The next day, my firstborn—a feisty, skinny newborn girl named Madelyn Ann—came wailing into the world and, for quite a while after, did not let up.

At the time Madelyn was born, my husband and I did not have much or really *any* experience with newborns. Although we read the books and took the childbirth classes, we were woefully unprepared for the first night of hell with our baby at home. She didn't cry—she screamed. Incessantly. Thanks to some La Leche influence, I was hellbent on breastfeeding, but my performance in that area was lacking. The hospital gave me a rubber shield to help with the process (after two days of trying, my nipples looked like they had been in a chemical accident). Breastfeeding by shield, I would come to find, was not nearly producing enough milk to satiate the baby.

At first, I thought all babies cried like Madelyn and resigned myself to accept the screaming as part of my new, yet horrific, normal. Then, I started talking with some other new moms. I learned their babies slept—slept!—hours at a time, with only occasional crying jags like the one my daughter was pitching at eight-hour clips. That's when I decided, to hell with this. I would be tortured no longer. We switched our daughter to formula and almost immediately the crying stopped. We began to enjoy, for the first time, the joy of our baby girl who was now wooing and no longer terrorizing us.

From then on, Madelyn Ann, our first born, was an easy child to raise in the sense that she mastered the potty, language, and math quickly, but she challenged the hell out of me on every and any other aspect. Like her mother (and grandmother), she is a voice for the underdog and a champion for the marginalized. Like her father, she is as steady and stubborn as a post, holding firmly to her convictions. An overachieving, classic "first child" archetype, Madelyn may have stopped screaming, but I know for sure she will never go quietly into this world.

By comparison, my second pregnancy hummed along mostly like the first—I welcomed back the elastic waist pants, flowy tops, naps, and comfort foods. Toward the final month of my second pregnancy, I do remember noticing a strange, yet can't-quite-put-my-finger-on-it change to my vision. When I found myself squinting while texting, I decided to make an appointment with an ophthalmologist. I've been blessed my whole life with 20/20 vision and the appointment found exactly that—perfect vision, nothing suspicious or remarkable about my eyes. All clear.

"Perhaps," they offered, "this is something related to the swelling or hormones from pregnancy. If something changes, give us a call."

Good enough for me, I thought; no need to panic.

Around the time of that appointment, I started experiencing

a tingling feeling that would run down the side of my left face. It almost felt like water trickling down the inside of my skull.

I mentioned this several times to my obstetricians during our routine check-ups. Believe it or not, I hadn't thought to *also* mention the change in vision. I simply hadn't put it together. Absent that information, they assumed—like me—this was simply a weird symptom of the pregnancy.

"Some women experience Bell's palsy with pregnancy," one of them shared. "It's not very common, but it does happen, and it usually goes away."

That seemed like a reasonable enough explanation for me and no need to worry now, I thought, since I was about to have a baby and any sort of invasive testing was probably off the table anyway. I started reading freakish stories like women who had entire ligaments go numb with pregnancy and that seemed to quell my anxiety.

Jameson Lee was born by C-section on October 27. Since we had scheduled the surgery, his birth was generally a relaxed experience. There was no rushing around, no fumbling with the phone to call my parents, no drama whatsoever. My husband and I arrived at the hospital at a crisp seven a.m. and the surgery went off without a hitch. I was shocked and marveled by how gentle Jameson came into the world. He barely cried for his first round of shots. He slept wonderfully and soundly in between feedings. By nearly all counts, he was—and still is—a more laid-back version of my husband and me. He is also sensitive to a fault, so he's careful with his heart, entrusting only a small circle of loved ones. He may never be the life of the party, but those whom he keeps in his circle will be lucky to earn a spot.

It was about six weeks after I delivered Jameson that I felt the first pangs of worry regarding my health. Feeling up to re-entry post-baby, I took my daughter to a local Christmas event in town. I remember squinting most of the drive there, trying to get the view into focus. About an hour into the event, walking felt more like stumbling with images overlapping one another like a kaleidoscope of moving pictures—buildings over sky, sidewalks over grass.

Since I didn't leave the house much (again, thanks to the distraction of the newborn), I waited until a week later to speak with my physician during my postpartum check-up. I remember we were finishing up my appointment before I mentioned anything.

"You and baby look great," my doctor beamed. "I think you're all set, then." She started to get up and gather her things.

"Yes, well, thank you," I said, slowly. "There is just this one thing I should mention before I go."

She sat back down and leaned in.

"I feel like my vision has changed."

"What do you mean exactly?" she asked.

"Well," I hesitated, "I—I'm kind of seeing double."

Her face fell and her eyes widened. "Are you serious?"

I felt guilty. I should have said something sooner.

"Yes," I said.

"For *how long*?" Now *she* seemed worried.

"It's been going on for a few weeks," I admitted.

She didn't hesitate. "We have to get you to a neurologist— like now."

Still not convinced this was anything other than something tied to my recent pregnancy, I went along with the neurology appointment the next day without much concern. I went through the motions like a good patient.

I remember doing acrobatic-like neuro tricks for the doctor. I seemed to be passing them all—touching my finger to my nose, tapping one foot, flipping my hand back and forth on my thigh, et cetera. We even cracked a few jokes.

But there was still that trouble with my vision. The nice doctor hemmed and hawed and thoughtfully asked me questions to see if there was something missing in the picture, something that could explain my condition.

"Have you felt dizzy? Any fainting? Headaches? How about migraines?"

"No, no, no and no."

Not coming up with anything substantial or concerning, he said an MRI would be able to tell us for sure what's happening. Even with this news, I was not worried. In fact, the only concern I had then was wrapping up the appointment so we could get to my daughter's daycare holiday party.

"Can the MRI wait till after Christmas?" I asked.

Afterall, it was only a week away.

"Oh, sure." He smiled back.

With that, we booked the MRI and a follow up visit after the new year. We then exchanged friendly wishes of a happy holiday season. "See you next year," we joked. That was the last time I saw that physician. The MRI would uncover a diagnosis far above the level of care he and his team could offer me.

With the hustle of the holidays over the next few days and the constant care and distraction of a newborn, I hardly gave another thought to what could be happening inside of me.

On December 25th, I was like any other exhausted, rundown, but elated mother of two young children on Christmas Day. With the secret, sneaking around (and expensive) shopping finally done, the gifts lovingly wrapped and mounded under the tree, the cookies baked and the meals prepped, cooked, and served, I finished the day with a glass of wine and a grateful heart.

I had a daughter, four, who still marveled at the magic of Christmas (while also being terrified of the Elf on a Shelf— an especially effective disciplinary tool that year). Asleep, rocking to whooshing sounds of his infant swing was my two-month-old son. He never fussed and slept perfectly. Our family felt balanced and wholly divine. As often happens in life, when I least suspected, the feeling of celebrating the holiest of holidays in the most perfect way was the proverbial calm before the storm that almost shattered my life.

I scheduled my brain MRI for the day after Christmas. I suppose I chose this day because I knew my husband wouldn't be working. (Like most women, I put others needs ahead of my own, not thinking for a second how the meaning of this day could forever impact my life should something disastrous be found.) I still believed, falsely, that my vision problems were tied to my recent pregnancy. I fully expected the MRI to come back clean and we'd be off to another round of tests until whatever was boiling beneath the surface eventually dried up and the symptoms would simply…go away. That was my thinking. That it would go away. It sounds careless now, but that was my rationale at the time.

My husband drove me to the hospital and escorted me through the registration process and back to the imaging suite. He kissed me good luck and said to call him when I was ready. I was greeted by the MRI technician. She was not unfriendly, but not kind either. She had bonfire red hair cropped short and wore hipster frames. She held a clipboard and fired off a few pre-screening questions without much eye contact. I know how shitty it is to work the day after Christmas (especially if you have kids), so I wasn't particularly offended by her crisp nature. She loaded me into the MRI and said she'd let me know when we were finished.

About five minutes later, I squeezed the emergency call bell to get the technician's attention. "Are we almost done?" I begged through the plastic shield covering my face. I was sure I could not take another minute in that torture chamber. I was wholly unprepared for the experience. I did not think to ask for—nor did they offer—a sedative or any comfort whatsoever. No warm blanket, no soft music, no Ativan, nothing. Just stone-cold sober me listening to the odd *whacks* and *clicks* and *thuds* of this cantankerous machine.

"Ma'am," the technician answered with a sigh, "you have four studies to go. We're not even a quarter through the first."

Jesus Christ. I couldn't believe it. How could they be so cruel? I endured the rest of the grueling MRI while half cursing the neurologist in my head and half clinging to any pictures of serenity my mind could conjure.

Two hours later, it was over. I felt like I just finished a marathon and immediately wept—loudly—over the horror of it all.

The technician was not impressed with my performance. There was no, "It will be okay," "You did great!" or "You should be so proud of yourself—that's not easy." Nothing remotely encouraging. Just, "The doctor will call you with the results."

With that, I was on my way. Still weeping, but grateful to be out of the cage. I thought for sure the worst was behind me.

Still rattled by the MRI, I came home shaky and anxious. About an hour after we were home, the phone rang. It was the neurologist's office.

"Hello?" I nearly yelled into the phone.

"Hi. I'm looking for Mrs. Tripp?" It was a female voice I didn't recognize.

"Yes, this is she."

"Hi, I'm calling from the neurologist's office—"

"Yes," I interrupted.

She introduced herself as the neurologist on call since the office was technically closed that day.

"Well, I don't know how much my colleague explained what could be causing your double vision, but it appears to be a sort of, well, glioma, on your brainstem."

She went on to say she had already put in a referral for an oncology visit and that I would be seen there very soon. "Probably on Monday."

Our conversation was over in a matter of minutes. The only question I recall asking was how to spell glioma. She had stopped me short at "oncology"—that word I definitely knew. To be fair, I hadn't met this physician before (remember, it was the day after Christmas and the office was closed, so she was on call for the physician with whom I'd done the neurology acrobats a few days previously). It's quite possible she has a lovely disposition for her "regular" patients. But one thing I've learned in this journey is that doctors generally are not good at breaking bad news. Read that again.

It's a lesson I wished I had learned on a much smaller scale (say, during treatment for a UTI or something), but I'm grateful to have learned it nonetheless.

There were a dozen questions that doctor could have asked to help brace me for the impact of her news.

"Are you alone?"

"Do you have someone with you?"

"Can you sit down for a moment?"

"Would you grab a pen and paper?"

Perhaps even, "Have you had any adult beverages yet today, Ms. Tripp?"

Any of the above would have helped soften the ground for a

devastating delivery.

Perhaps doctors feel ashamed to give patients bad news. After all, they've taken an oath on their profession. Maybe, on some level, they view it as a professional failure—odd as it may sound—to announce unpleasant outcomes. Certainly not all doctors fail in this regard (I have since had fantastic encounters with other physicians). Still, I know for sure when this particular physician was in the position to communicate a life-altering diagnosis, she clearly and unequivocally failed. She did not offer comfort, support, or gauge in anyway my ability to absorb the information in that moment. I never spoke to that physician again either (she was just the "on call" doc, after all), but I hope another patient or their loved one spoke up where I was silent. It's simply too important to get wrong.

Like a bad patient, I saved all my questions for Google and began to "me-search" my diagnosis. Search results for "brainstem glioma" revealed that the brainstem (also called the "pons") controls automatic bodily functions for survival like blood pressure and breathing. A glioma is a type of tumor often located in the brain. On average, patients diagnosed with a brainstem glioma, I learned, can expect to live ten months to a year. This vicious tumor is aggressive, inoperable and 100% incurable. I was stunned and terrified at what my internet searches uncovered. Still, there was a small voice inside me that offered a line from my beloved *The Divine Comedy*, a piece I studied in college. When Dante finally reunites with his dearly departed Beatrice in Paradiso (heaven) and begins to weep, she tells him, "Do not yet weep, do not weep yet; you'll need your tears for what another sword must yet inflict."

With Beatrice's advice in mind, I pulled myself together and blocked out the Internet scares. I felt, again, that somehow, someway, my story could be written differently. My extended family and I (yes, my husband, mother, father, and newborn in tow) marched onward and into my first oncology appointment. This would become the base of my first Kilimanjaro, the proverbial mountain I had to climb to reach the summit and face the storm before the rainbow could emerge.

We have your results

If you are awaiting medical results that could result in a life-changing diagnosis, here are a few tips to prepare for the news.

1. When you receive the call, immediately ask if a loved one should be included in the conversation before any results are shared.

2. Ask to take a moment to grab a pencil/pen and paper before going further in the conversation.

3. Have them spell any key terms and don't forget to ask for their name and title. Write everything down.

4. Do not let them make you feel rushed. You are the patient, and you have the right to ask as many questions about your health as necessary.

5. Always ask if you have any restrictions at this time. You don't know what you don't know.

"Unless they can look into the core of your heart, and see the degree of your passion, or look into the depths of your soul and see the extent of your will, then they have no business telling you what you can or cannot achieve. While they may know the odds, they do not know you."

- Sandra Kring"

Chapter 4
The Year of the Patient

Given the three facts you just read about my tumor (aggressive, inoperable, incurable), you can imagine my surprise when the oncologist welcomed us in the most jovial of spirits. He was upbeat and exceptionally personable, teasingly calling us "the von Trapp family" (from the *Sound of Music*). He seemed genuine in his questions and even cracked jokes to lighten our collective heavy mood.

I remember one of the first things he did was take my pulse.

"I'm alive," I said. "That's a pretty good start."

"Hey, I'm the doctor here," he jibed back with a smirk.

We continued the exam with more jovial exchanges and then he started getting to the business of my health.

"How have you been feeling?"

"When did you first notice the double vision?"

"Tell me about your family history," and so forth.

Then it was time to excuse my parents, to allow space for a physical exam.

"Oh, sure, sure. Of course," they offered as they scrambled to lift their things (plus the newborn) and hustle out of the exam room.

I went through the same neuro-acrobats I had gone through with the neurologist.

"Follow my finger."

"Close your eyes and touch your nose."

"Walk forward and backward."

With the relaxed banter and standard doctor-patient questioning, perhaps, I considered at the time, this wasn't the doomsday scenario the Internet had painted. Looking back, I know we needed the doctor's levity. It was almost too grim a scenario for anyone to bear. Here I was, a young mother with her newborn sleeping in his carrier, trying to look pulled together while my face twisted with worry and confusion. To this day, I also wonder if it was the physician's own anxiety or nervousness about my case that precipitated a sort of "acting out" with upbeat humor replacing grave concern. I'm still not sure. Like other unusual stops I've passed along my climb, I'll never know. After a few exercises, he waved my parents back into the exam room.

"I want you to see a neurooncologist," he decided. "We have a very good one in town, and we'll see if he can see you this week." He started doling handshakes and goodbyes when I interrupted him.

"Actually," I said. "I have a question before you go."

He stopped, turned, and sat back down.

"On a scale of one to five," I asked, "how serious is this?"

Without much hesitation, his wise-guy smile dropped, and his eyes lowered. "I'd say it's a four-something."

Doctors are not good at giving bad news. Once again, here was the lesson I learned during what I would later term, "The Year of the Patient." It was a year I spent struggling against the friction of a broken, busted, and fried healthcare system (and this was before the COVID-19 pandemic).

To our surprise, the local neurooncologist was able to see me later that same day. Wonderful. My mother, husband, and I headed over after lunch. We were registered right away and immediately taken back to his exam room. Then, we waited for what felt like an eternity before someone finally knocked on the door. "Come in," we all yelled.

In strutted a whole Andy Kauffman-era, artsy postmodern vibe. Dressed in cowboy boots, tight pastel slacks, a sharp dress shirt, a designer sportscoat, and John Lennon-like frames, the neurooncologist extended his hand and welcomed me to his clinic. He whispered when he spoke and paced his words carefully and steadily, commanding an intense aura around him.

"If everyone had to have a brain tumor," he began, "they would line up behind you." He went on to theorize the tumor had likely occurred when I was a small child and something (we don't know what) put the brakes on it. Only recently, he guessed, had it started to regrow. It may or may not have been related to either or both pregnancies. It was impossible to know for sure.

"Is this a death sentence for me?" I wanted—but also didn't want—to know. I'm certain he sensed my fear.

After some moments of silent, steady thinking, he offered, "Anything but." Still, he recommended I seek a second opinion from a more sophisticated healthcare system. A place that sees "this type of mutation" every day. He offered to phone a colleague in New York to get me in to a renowned medical facility. Later that evening, he called me at home to say my appointment was all set—thanks to a few favors he phoned in to the clinic.

A week later, my husband and I took the Megabus to New York City for an overnight trip. I was scheduled to see a top-ranked physician at the medical center. This visit, like many stops along the Year of the Patient, did not go as planned. At the appointment, I spent more time with a medical resident than the physician. Since I expected my care plan to be uniquely crafted to me, I went into great detail on everything from my great-uncle's weird mole to my unusually aggressive form of chicken pox as a child. I left no medical stone unturned. When the doctor finally did arrive for my visit, she was harried and largely dismissive.

"What brings you here today?" she asked as she washed her hands.

Are you effing serious? I thought but didn't say aloud. Instead, I provided a more succinct version of my medical history, the vision trouble, the neurology, the MRI, and the neurooncologist. "So that's why I'm here," I finished.

After hearing all this, she seemed confused and asked why I would come all the way to New York for a visit when my diagnosis was clear, and the treatment options were limited. I couldn't tell if I was a lost cause, an anomaly, or if this was a cut and dry cancer case, no fancy extra referrals needed.

"Well, let me examine you," she offered.

I guess she felt obligated to do *something* with me. After all, I had come all this way. We ran through the same neuro-acrobats I did with the neurologist.

"What questions do you have for me?" she asked.

"What do you think is my prognosis?" I cut right to it. A question for the ages.

Her eyebrows twisted and she bit her lip, looking at me sympathetically.

"Will—will this kill me?" I asked.

"Certainly not," is what I expected her to say, hoping the findings of my early internet searches were largely exaggerated or completely false.

"Oh my, yes," is what she actually said, most definitively.

"How long? When?" I pressed her for answers.

"Well, I—I don't know. But the empirical research shows…" she muttered.

"Ten years?" I interrupted.

"No, not that long."

"Five years?"

"I—I simply don't have a crystal ball…but the data suggests a couple years."

Holy shit.

"I was told this was not a death sentence," I thought aloud, recalling my visit with the neurooncologist.

"It's not…in the sense that you only have days or months to live, but this is a terminal illness. I'm sorry if your doctors didn't explain that to you."

You're sorry? No, I'm sorry. I'm sorry I took time I didn't have away from my family to come to this stupid clinic, I thought. I'm sorry I expected more sympathy. More compassion. I had imagined this to be a full day's visit, complete with nutritionists and bloodwork, scans, and a total neurooncological workup. Perhaps also a yogi or reiki session followed by a couple's massage. Instead, it was over in fifteen minutes. There was no spiritual coach, no wellness partner—no goddamn herbal tea. Just *good luck* and a business card. It was maddening but, more than anything, I felt completely defeated. I sunk in the exam chair feeling invisible and utterly powerless under the neon lights of an exam room housed within one of the best cancer centers in the world.

Already checked out of our hotel, my husband and I now had seven hours to kill before the Megabus ride home. We shuffled through the city on a brutally cold January day. I called my oncologist and neurooncologist from a McDonald's. They were disappointed, but not totally surprised at the outcome of the visit. I, however, felt foolish, betrayed, and broken.

Forget this not being the news I was expecting—this was not the *life* I was expecting. I had enjoyed, up to this point, a relatively uneventful life. From my perspective, albeit biased, I was an easy kid to raise. I rarely spoke out of turn and never got into trouble. I worked my ass off in college, spending an inordinate amount of time in the library. I graduated summa cum laude from my undergraduate and graduate degree programs. I had a savings account. I recycled and upcycled when I could. I went to church. I volunteered. I practiced yoga. I kept the faith. I did all the things right in a future-focused mindset now wiped in a matter of fifteen minutes. My mind reeled through the moments I would miss— retirement, birthdays, graduations, grandchildren—all stolen from my cerebral hope chest. With the physician's prognosis (death in a couple years) ringing in my ears, the world fell beneath my feet and, despite all the signs leading up to this moment, I still had not seen it coming.

When we got home, we started making calls to other cancer centers: Duke, Mayo Clinic, and Johns Hopkins among those I recall. We learned a biopsy would be the only way to determine the exact DNA of my tumor, which would help to identify the best treatment plan and better predict my prognosis. The treatment plan was especially critical because, I learned, there is a lifetime limit on how much radiation one can safely receive to certain parts of the body. In my case, I was told that I had one shot at treatment. If the radiation successfully shrunk the tumor but it regrew, I would not be able to receive radiation treatment to that area again. With chemotherapy ruled ineffective at reaching the tumor and surgery not being an option due to the location and presence of the tumor (rather than a solid mass, it weaved in and out of healthy cells, making it virtually impossible to remove), radiation therapy was my only viable treatment option, and there was no margin for error. My physician was careful that this would treat, but not cure, the cancer. After some significant prayer and deliberation (also against the advice of my neurooncologist), I scheduled a brainstem biopsy with a gregarious Greek neurosurgeon in Baltimore. It was a miracle to find him—most physicians wouldn't dare operate near the brainstem. I'd been told it was too dangerous an area to go poking around in. This physician, however, successfully operated on brainstem patients regularly—myself now included.

Everyone was nervous about me having the biopsy.

My neurooncologist warned, "You can go through with this and get answers, but you may never be the same again."

All options, including the risk of death, were on the table for anything that could go wrong during the procedure. There was something about this physician, though, that made me confident in my choice to go forward anyway. I felt this when my mother and I spoke to him on the phone prior to my surgery. He could have rattled off his prestige, board certified training, and internationally respected reputation to assuage my mother's fears as she continued to present them.

Instead, he took a kinder, more accessible road. "I understand, Mom," he said in his thick Greek accent.

I loved that he called my mom, "Mom."

"I have daughter too and I would have same concerns as you. I assure you that we take very good care of daughter. Daughter will be okay. Daughter needs this information for her health. I will not let you down, Mom."

With that, in late February, my husband and I hit the road again, this time traveling to Maryland for my brainstem biopsy. Still going through the motions of survival, I had not prepared myself for the aftermath of the surgery. Afterward, I was placed immediately in the ICU, then the neurosurgery tower for close monitoring. Eventually, I was able to have liquids, then some solids, then some time upright in my bed. When they asked me to try walking, the connections from my brain to my legs were frayed. It was exhausting to climb out of bed—with the assistance of my husband and two nurses—but eventually, I stood, then walked before collapsing again back into bed. This pattern continued for quite a while until I was strong enough to be transported safely home, thirteen staples in my head and feeling as though I had been rescued from a prisoner camp.

While grueling, the biopsy unlocked the precise nature of my tumor (a grade II astrocytoma, diffuse pontine glioma), which helped to craft an exactly right radiation plan. Now knowing just what we were dealing with, I felt emboldened to continue my journey through treatment, healing, and eventually, yes—remission.

In March, I met with my local hospital's radiation oncologist, who introduced me to a physicist in charge of mapping out my radiation based on the images produced by the MRI along with an all-star team of techs—seasoned pros who would be with me during each and every treatment. The first order of business was molding a plastic cage that was an exact replica of my face; this would be clamped over me during treatments. This was to keep my head still so that the radiation delivered with pinpoint precision. I lied on an exam table as they tilted me all the way back, at a 180-degree angle and proceeded to pour warm, melted plastic on my face. I can't recall how long it took to wait as the plastic set, but I do remember it being the first time I employed a guided imagery coping mechanism.

As the plastic cooled and settled, I closed my eyes (partly pretending I was enjoying a facial) and transported to the back porch swing at my grandma Marge's house. I could feel the breeze as I rocked myself back and forth while lying down, barefoot and legs crossed under a crocheted throw. I could hear the chirps, motoring engines, and occasional screen door slams of suburbia. I could feel the cool metal of the swing's chains on my fingers and toes. I did not expect this particular image to emerge in my mind rather than a million other Zen-like places (white beaches, waterfall parks, infinity pools, or sprawling emerald rolling hills, for example) until I realized it was not an image but a memory. One that I associated with childhood, warmth, and calm—my proverbial "safe place." The memory became a treasure during my cancer climb. I encourage everyone to mine their memories for a moment—the simpler and more tactical, the better—and let it be a touchstone for safety during life's turbulence. The power it holds for centering oneself in the storm is simply amazing.

Every day for thirty-six days, my safe place carried me through hour-long radiation sessions. These sessions began with the radiation technicians helping me lie on a table. Once I was lying flat, they'd place the plastic mask atop my face. To keep me still during the radiation treatments, they bolted the mask (and, effectively, me) to the table.

Once they had me precisely positioned, I was left alone while the linear accelerator (the radiation beaming device) rotated around me, delivering invisible medicine to stop and shrink the growth of my tumor. I always closed my eyes during the treatments and stayed safely in my mind swaying on the porch swing.

You do not feel or smell the radiation as it's delivered, but over time you do wear from its cumulative dosage—exhaustion is its hallmark symptom. Another symptom, one I hadn't quite planned for, is hair loss. In my case it was possible, but not guaranteed, that I would lose my hair from the radiation treatments.

About halfway through my treatment cycle (around week three), that changed. I was in the shower shampooing my hair when clumps—not strands—loosely tumbled into my hands. It was one of the lowest points in my cancer journey. Research has demonstrated that women find hair loss to be the most devasting symptom of cancer treatment, even worse than losing a breast. For me and for most patients, I would argue it's the loss of identity, not *hair*, that sends you reeling from feeling utterly powerless.

In the end, I did lose and eventually regrew most of my hair. I've kept it pixie-length since. This being an act that is equal parts gender norm defiance and protection against the potential sting of another moment in the shower watching my identity circle the drain. There are some things even a safe place cannot help.

To be sure, I had my share of emotional spiraling during treatment. I recall, vividly, a nightly routine of lying on my closet floor weeping while clutching one of my daughter's shirts against my face. There was no way, I felt, to atone for why this was happening to me. Rocking and weeping, weeping and rocking, nothing and no one at the time could pull me out of my sorry state, until one day, another part of me spoke up. I'm not sure if it was the voice of my guardian angel, the depths of my soul, or another spiritual presence but it spoke clearly and definitively. The voice offered a deal, a survival mechanism of sorts. I was allowed to feel sorry for myself, but the crying fits had to stop. I could not continue these tantrums, hiding in that closet, wasting another precious moment wallowing in my hardship.

From that day forward, I made a pact with the voice (and, for good measure, God). As long as I could stop my wallowing, I would be here long enough to raise my children. I always believed my essential job as a mother was to teach my children how to survive in a world without me, and if I could do that, I would be okay. Deal. While I've been tempted many times to stray, I've kept my word and, so far, He (the voice) has kept His.

After my radiation treatments were over, an MRI revealed my tumor had shrunk significantly. "Now comes the hard part," my radiation physician shared. He went on to explain while the treatments were largely successful, I would need to be placed in permanent observation status (meaning, I would need to meet with my neurooncologist and have routine, serial MRIs).

Six months later, I began a twice annual routine of slipping into the MRI (now with a sedative and warm blanket), heading into the clinic the next day and waiting to hear if I had six more months to live or prepare to die based on the results of the imaging. Mercifully, each time, I learned the tumor continued to stay dormant (essentially, unchanged), which was exceptional news. Then, I would always end the visit by posing the same question I asked at the start of my climb, "What is my prognosis?"

After I had a few follow-up appointments under my belt, I started to probe for a ballpark, a guesstimate – anything to give me hope beyond just the next half a year. Each time, it was a different but similar play on the theme of, "we don't know for sure, but for now you are OK." Sadly, no one ever said the words

I really *wanted* to hear: "you will be OK." In the absence of this consolation, the visits left me feeling defeat, pity, and sadness. Then, something changed.

About two years after my treatment, during one of my "routine," post-MRI visits, I asked again, "what is my prognosis?"

After a brief pause, the physician smiled and said, "Unknown."

That was a pivotal moment in my journey. Unknown. I had never considered that option, but I liked it. Unknown offered hope. Unknown meant possibility. Unknown, for me, was a welcome—even exciting—new choice.

While, of course, I would prefer to be declared cancer free, unknown sounded better because it did not have an expiration date. With the help of relaxers and warm blankets, over time the follow-up MRIs became a breeze. The lead up to the twice annual and now annual neurooncologist have become less anxiety-ridden over time. Even in the less than perfect places, I remind myself I am lucky to have these moments; far too many will never get there, taken from disease or other tragic intervention. Fact is, no matter our diagnosis, we all have the same prognosis: unknown. At the time of my diagnosis, my mother predicted that many would go before me. She was right. I've seen colleagues, friends, neighbors, and family members alike leave their earthly journeys—some expected, but most not. When tragedies occur, it reaffirms for me that nothing is guaranteed except this present moment. With that knowledge, my expectations shifted, and lessons learned, I had climbed to the top and could safely descend to the base of my first Kilimanjaro and into the unknown.

The Art of Guided Imagery

While it may sound intimidating, guided imagery is simply about focusing on images, sounds and/or sensations to help calm you. I think of it as intentional daydreaming. Guided imagery is a powerful tool that has been associated with vast health benefits, notably for cancer patients.

Since this technique works best when all five senses are engaged, I encourage you to mine your heart for a happy memory that is so vivid you can actually feel the weather or the clothes you were wearing just as sure as you know how this page will feel on your fingers.

Close your eyes, breathe deeply and replay this memory as often as you need to center yourself and your thoughts until you become still. Sit with that peace for a few moments and repeat as needed.

"The good physician treats the disease; the great physician treats the patient who has the disease."

- Sir William Osler

Chapter 5

The Healthcare Curve

Aside from my pregnancies, annual check-ups, and a few questionable moles, like most people, before my diagnosis, I did not have much experience in serious healthcare matters; no sprains, fractures, or life-threatening injuries to my name. To be sure, 2015 (aka "The Year of the Patient," as I would come to call it) would prove to offer my most intense interactions with healthcare.

For full disclosure, I should mention when I received my diagnosis, I was about ten years into what would become a nearly fifteen-year career in healthcare. In 2014 (the year of my diagnosis), I was employed by a mid-sized healthcare system as a marketing manager. I entered the healthcare field in 2007, about two years after I finished graduate school, when I accepted a position as a writing/editing specialist for a small healthcare system in eastern Pennsylvania. I was enthralled by the work. Any day could be spent attending a glitzy photo shoot, interviewing a high-profile patient, observing open-heart surgery, or writing epic speeches for a rather grand-standing CEO. I loved the challenges of "marketing" healthcare and finding ways to cleverly package its best offerings to consumers.

The industry felt, at that time, seductive and flashy. New technologies, revolutionary medicines, and the beginnings of real patient advocacy were creating the perfect storm of radical change and forcing the industry to adopt a more consumer-focused marketing mindset than ever before. It was a wild and exciting time to be a part of the business.

Since I spent much of my career touting the finest the industry had to offer, I brought high expectations to my patient experiences. That, in combination with inheriting an Italian short fuse and sense of righteousness, made for a powerful punch on patient advocacy.

Sometimes, my expectations were met, even exceeded. Other times, however, they fell extraordinarily short.

An executive at a former health system I worked for once shared a most fitting analogy for the healthcare experience—one that, to this day, I still find myself repeating. For healthcare workers (both clinical and non-clinical professionals alike), our days spent working in the field are mostly black and white. Days run together, weeks turn into months, and years come and go as we trek on through our routines and daily grinds. Our patients, however, are another story; their healthcare experiences are seen in vivid color. They may have been preparing for days, weeks, or even months for their visits. They will notice and remember—at times, with focused and sharp precision—the good, bad, and simply ugly moments that may happen as part of their interactions with healthcare.

There were certainly moments I experienced all the above throughout my journey. I think back to the initial call when I received my diagnosis and my visit to New York City. Both high-impact, life-changing moments were marked not with compassion or empathy but with sterility and brevity. The physicians seemed agitated and strained to get on with their next task. In both cases, I should have felt like the most important person in the room, commanding full attention and support of the care team. Instead,

I felt like a nobody—an insignificant (and inconvenient) blip in their otherwise black and white day. When they were finished with me, they would go back to fighting with the odd complexities of their electronic medical record system or chasing insurance companies on patient care denials. The business of healthcare was getting in the way of the delivery of medicine. I knew it. They knew it. And, I'm sure other patients *felt* it.

After my brainstem biopsy, when I was bed-ridden in the ICU, my memory of that experience is fuzzy, but I recall pointed moments where I felt frustrated and, frankly, ignored by the staff. I had nurses dart in and out of my room without introducing themselves or bothering to explain what they were fiddling with in my IV. I had asked repeatedly, then begged, for help with my right eye, which had been inadvertently scratched during the surgery. It felt like an eternity before I received relief (it came only after I demanded a second opinion from the nurse who was too harried to slow down and exam my eye). I pleaded for ice chips, and I remember being so thirsty at some point that it actually hurt. After being transferred to the neurosurgery tower, I could hear a gaggle of staff laughing and bullshitting about their weekend plans outside my room in the middle of the night while

I was trying to rest after an exhausting, painful day. When I was well enough to be discharged, my social worker had the audacity to complain about her day and blamed other staff members for "the wait" as we were held up until they gathered my discharge documents (my husband and I were trying to get on the road home ahead of an impending snowstorm). When we finally did receive my paperwork, she disagreed with my follow-up care and threatened the possibility of developing deep vein thrombosis (a blood clot) if I did not heed her advice of wearing compression stockings even though the discharge instructions said otherwise. Even in my sickest, weakest state, I could feel these friction points, which did not at all match the masterful work of my neurosurgeon. Once again, I had the privilege of receiving care in one of the world's finest healthcare facilities, yet I did not feel seen or heard as a patient, much less a person.

Opposite that feeling, yet equally jarring, was an experience I had about two years post-treatment when I received TME (too much emotion). I was checking out from a routine follow-up visit with my neurooncologist.

"When should we schedule you to come back?" the receptionist asked, smiling behind her glasses.

"Six months," I said.

"Really?" She seemed genuinely surprised but also skeptical. "Are you sure?"

I looked behind me to see if she was perhaps speaking to someone else. "I'm sorry, what?" I asked.

"Well, usually when it says this," she whispered as she pointed to the word *malignant* on my chart, "we don't tend to see you back."

Granted, this woman wasn't trying to be unkind. She seemed genuinely delighted at the possibility of not having to see "yet another" patient's obituary in the paper.

But that was her experience, *her* feelings. She had no regard for how terrifying it was for me, the patient, to hear her say something like that. Patients are vulnerable and tortured enough; there's no need to editorialize their journey, no matter how pleasantly surprised you are to hear they will be back, not *dead*, in the next six months. I ignored her comments and continued to book the next visit, pretending this exchange was not wildly inappropriate.

When you have a serious diagnosis, you tend to become highly paranoid of your body. Even the slightest ache or discomfort can shoot you down a rabbit hole of worry. Such was the case when I met with an otolaryngology doctor to examine my throat. I had started noticing that my voice would crackle randomly on occasion, and I was worried the radiation had passed through my larynx and was causing problems (this was about six months after my radiation treatments).

After reviewing my medical history, the physician asked me, rather pointedly, "How big was your tumor?"

My eyes widened and searched the ceiling for an answer. "I— I don't really know."

"You don't *know*?" he asked, incredulously.

"No. I don't think I'd want to know," I said, now on my heels. "Would you want to know?" I shot back. "If it were you?"

He looked at me and said, "Yes, of course," without hesitation.

I snapped back, "Well, yeah. That's because you're a doctor." (Read: you're also somewhat psychotic).

He continued with the visit and stepped out to get his equipment. "Three centimeters," he said when he came back. "Your tumor was three centimeters." He had taken the liberty of doing some research in my medical chart.

I looked down and nodded.

He lectured me on the importance of "looking out for myself," "being my own advocate," and really "understanding my disease." "Keep it real," he said. "You have children, after all."

He wasn't wrong—every patient has the right and responsibility to be educated about their condition. But here's something he hadn't considered: One of the body's great tricks is its ability to block certain events after a trauma.

As Darren Strauss writes in his memoir *Half a Life*: "The truth about shock and about our bodies is that they don't want us to feel things deeply. We're designed to act, react, forget; to be shallow."

Now, I'm sure I was told the size of my tumor—likely more than once. I had seen pictures of it on a computer screen (again, more than once). My instincts had simply blocked the details so I couldn't dwell on, wallow in, or picture the size of the horrifying glitch in my brain. I wasn't a negligent patient or a bad mother. I was a survivor. A *trauma* survivor. Make no mistake, a cancer journey is a traumatic one, and the corresponding triggers and proactive stabilizers the body invents are very real. Still, the sting of the physician's judgment stayed with me years after the appointment (for the record, my throat was fine, and I *still* don't think about the size of the tumor).

As I said earlier, not all my patient experiences were bad. I remember a fabulous interaction I had with a local eye doctor shortly after my diagnosis but before the biopsy. I had started wearing an eye patch, which seemed to help with my double vision. It worked, but I wasn't sure if that was the right thing to do. Is there one eye I should patch all the time? Or none of the time? Would it affect my other eye by making it work harder? I met with this physician to discuss the above (and, likely, a million other questions). He had a grandfatherly like appearance—white hair, bushy eyebrows, and an argyle sweater vest. I don't recall all we discussed in that visit, but I do remember him sitting across from me, taking his left hand, and placing it just atop my right elbow.

He squeezed gently and said, "May I just say that I am so sorry for you."

It was the first time a healthcare provider had expressed understanding and, moreover, genuine compassion for my diagnosis. I will never forget that moment of simple, human kindness.

It's a timeworn act ironically too often forgotten in today's high-pressure healthcare industry, where a nurse performs, on average, seventy-two tasks an hour and physicians are compensated increasingly more for quantity over quality of care.

For far too long, I believe, patients have graded healthcare on a curve. They have tolerated long hold times on the phone, curt receptionists, communication rifts among disparate electronic medical records, rude clinicians deemed to have "poor bedside manners," along with confusing, and for some, debt-inducing billing statements all because the healthcare industry gets a pass to misbehave.

Thanks to market disrupters like on-demand point of care apps and retail-based clinics, the curve is getting shorter. With more options, consumers are simply growing less tolerant of bad behaviors. With the Amazon-like expectations of today's younger generations, within the not-too-distant future, I predict the curve will likely be shortened even more until it is altogether gone.

Simply put, patients are consumers and vice versa; there is no hardline between those worlds and its shared experiences. The faster healthcare systems catch up with this, the better positioned they will be to serve and survive the saturated healthcare market in the future. And the better served their patients will be—they should and can "have it all." That means the best technology delivered on the patient's time at the price they desire in the manner that makes them feel seen, validated, and heard.

Of course, there are still clinicians who celebrate and rally for their patients. One inspiring example from my journey was a vision therapist I worked with after my radiation treatment to course-correct my double vision. While other providers warned the nerve damage by my tumor was irreversible and that I should expect my vision to remain unchanged, my sweet therapist said anything but. Perhaps it was because she was used to working with pediatric patients or maybe it was due to her genuinely kind spirit, but either way, her unwavering support and determination to improve my vision was the spectacular cheerleading I didn't know I needed.

For the first time since diagnosis, my confidence and spirits lifted because of her support. "Good, that's *very* good," she praised, beaming ear to ear after I completed even the simplest of tasks.

My eyes strained to see certain objects correctly—double vision was still affecting me daily and was a symptom I was warned would not cease, even after radiation treatment. Still, we persisted through months of vision therapy. By our last session, my vision had markedly improved. I still had moments of double vision, but it was not nearly as often or as debilitating as it had been previously. Before I left our last session, I remember saying a tearful goodbye to my vision therapist and thanking her for giving me back my life.

I don't know if she entirely understood the compliment or the gravity of her effect on my healing. The vision therapy clinic did not have AI machines, sci-fi robotics, or clinically trialed medicine. My therapist had the necessary tools and the heart of a champion. Far from the "nobody treatment," I always felt like the only patient and the highest priority.

Without knowing it, that clinic and that therapist were changing the bar in healthcare delivery and expectation. Practitioners like my vision therapist do not need a curve because there are no hiccups to atone for; they simply get it right by treating patients kindly, appropriately, and with the highest degree of integrity along every step of the patient's journey, delivering a quality, friction-less experience that stays with the patient long after a tearful goodbye.

Patient vulnerability

I believe it is too often forgotten how woefully vulnerable patients become. Being admitted to a hospital is not unlike being processed for prison:

- You surrender all your belongings into a plastic bag.
- You change into a drab uniform.
- You are at the mercy of others' time, attitudes, and attention.
- You are not in control.
- Your schedule is set for you.
- You are scared.
- You are sick.
- You are lonely.
- You are at the mercy of those who choose to show kindness.
- The employees have all the power; you only have your underwear.*

***Edit:** You actually have more. You have a voice and a right to advocate for your needs and hold those accountable for what will become a life-altering (and expensive) transaction. You may not know healthcare, but you DO know what dignity, compassion, and kindness feels like, and those values are powerful medicines in the healing process.

"When you come to the edge of all of the light you've known, and are about to step off into the darkness of the unknown; faith is knowing one of two things will happen. You'll have something solid to stand on, or you'll be taught how to fly."

- Patrick Overton

Chapter 6
Reeling in Remission

I was at a party recently talking to an old colleague. She had shared that her husband had a cancer diagnosis in his early twenties. I hadn't known this all that time we had worked together.

"I'm so sorry," I offered.

"Thanks," she said bashfully, "but, it's okay. If he gets a good check-up this year, he'll have made it to the nine-year mark."

"Oh?" I asked. "What happens then?"

"Essentially, she shared, "he's declared cancer-free, and the monitoring is no longer needed. In other words, they can stop worrying about it."

Now, I know everyone's cancer journey is different, but that was a radical statement to me. In nine years, they'd no longer have to worry about it? Sure, I understand that worry never truly ends once a cancer diagnosis is made, but the idea of not having to go through the medical rigmarole was unimaginable. No more needles, no more waiting, no more imaging tubes?

I'm thrilled they have this possibility but it's a bitter temptation in my world. Sadly, other than death, there are no milestones or anniversaries that will mark the end of my cancer journey. It will always be in my life even when its growth is at bay.

It wasn't until I was completing my medical leave paperwork to take time off for radiation therapy that the reality of its permanency hit. In the field indicated for noting the "duration of condition," my oncologists scribbled: "lifetime." The words felt so heavy, like a boulder had just sunk in my lap. I'd been sentenced to life. Not months or years—but life.

The best I could hope for in my journey was that the radiation would shrink and slow the tumor from growing. It *would* grow back, but the hope was the growth would be extraordinarily slow. My brainstem biopsy revealed the glioma had an extraordinary slow growth rate (less than 1%), which was heartening to learn when compared to the vicious growth rate of other, more aggressive brain tumors like a glioblastoma. It was still frightening to imagine the way in which the tumor could mutate and become a more aggressive, faster growing cancer over time. There was also the undisputed evidence that demonstrated pontine gliomas have a zero percent survival rate with most patients only seeing a few years past initial diagnosis. Still, I was prognosis: unknown, and I had to remember that I was, effectively, on par with everyone else in the grand scheme of the universe.

After post-treatment scans revealed the tumor had gone months, then years, without any change, I was officially declared to be in remission. This would put me at the base of my second Kilimanjaro, alas the second sword Beatrice predicted.

With remission, I felt grateful but not liberated. Even with the blessing of remission, the ghost of uncertainty would come to terrorize me. At times, I felt as though I were living with a loaded gun to my temple—cocked and ready, just a finger flick away from firing. I imagine other patients must feel this way even after a successful cancer treatment; a period otherwise known as "remission," when the signs of disease have been reduced or removed.

Sadly, I came to learn it's not just the disease that recedes. The support that comes with a cancer journey also fades around this time. That was hard for me to accept. People's lives simply moved on with time. Some got married or divorced; others grew their families or moved to new towns for new jobs. Still stuck in the shock of cancer, I had not braced myself for the reality of others' journeys. Surely, I didn't expect lasagnas and casseroles to appear at my door forever or handwritten notes to be part of my daily mail collection. However, I was not ready to accept the world would hum along while I felt immobilized.

The Greek root for remission is *remit*, which means "to forgive or to pardon." I felt neither. At times, I still felt betrayed by my own body and, more often, by God. On low days, I found myself asking the question, "*Why* did this happen to *me*?" What had I done to receive such torture—on my body, on my mind…on my heart? Facing these questions was as painful as they were unanswerable. I believe this is why I developed, and still hold, a distinct disliking for the association of the word "remission" with terms like, "winning," as in, "She *won* her battle with cancer." Or (more often the case) losing, as in, "She *lost* her battle with cancer" (the way far too many obituaries begin). No one wins or loses to cancer because it's not a fair fight. Two relatively alike individuals with the same diagnosis and treatment could have totally disparate outcomes.

Moreover, framing a cancer death as a "loss" assumes the person gave up or, by their own fault, just somehow couldn't overcome the disease. This is just my opinion, of course, but from the perspective of someone who's looked down the barrel, I would challenge the use of the term "winner" and "loser" when describing any cancer patient, deceased or alive. I believe you are no more a winner in remission than you are a loser in recurrence. Labeling patients in this way isn't fair to them and it certainly isn't an accurate representation of a cancer journey.

While living in the purgatory of remission (not sick yet not well) I developed other new triggers that provoked odd behaviors in myself I didn't recognize or realize were happening until I had the benefit of time and reflection.

About a year after I returned to work, our well-liked CEO announced he would be retiring in the next six months. When I first heard this news, my reaction wasn't any different than most around me; I felt surprised and a little disappointed but certainly not devastated. When I attended his farewell reception, however, I made the first of what would become several embarrassing emotional displays fueled by a sense of abandonment. Small feelings of sadness were replaced with an overwhelming wave of grief. While others offered friendly handshakes and well wishes, I wept (seemingly inexplicably) at his leaving. I thought this was because I associated the CEO with the job I also linked to my pre-cancer life; his leaving, I hypothesized at the time, symbolized the passing of some of the final remnants of my "old" life.

When I was triggered in a similar way by others who moved on to retirements, new jobs, or promotions, I realized the common denominators in these scenarios were "change" and "me." I was the one who became upset when others moved on because, on some level, my psyche had associated the feeling of change with cancer. Any change in my life, even and especially when it involved others who had supported me during my diagnosis and treatment, triggered feelings of betrayal and raw vulnerability. I would be brought immediately back to the early days in my cancer journey when moments of despair and heartache quite literally floored me.

It took years to unlock this association but once I held the key, I could better prepare and therefore stabilize myself in a way that prevented emotional breakdowns where none should occur. Like most self-revelations, reflection and the grace of time helped me to understand the impetus behind my behaviors.

After years of analysis, therapy, and emotional deep diving, I learned this to be my most intense trigger from cancer. There were and are still others I'm working on, but knowing this about myself was far and away the greatest blessing to come from the benefit of quiet, inward retrospection that it seems only devastation can bring upon ourselves.

While I was not one to attend a support group, it did help me to hear from other trauma survivors. And, I found them in unexpected places. An article I had read years prior to my cancer journey – and then revisited after treatment – provided surprising comfort as I navigated the assimilation from my sick to well-but-not cured self. In an article titled, "I Will Never Know Why," originally published in *O, The Oprah Magazine* (November 2009), Susan Klebold unpacks her emotional spiraling after her son, Dylan, and his friend had (now infamously) carried out a deadly mass shooting at Columbine High School. In her quest to understand, on some level, how this could have possibly happened, she pivots the conversation from the usual topics of parenting, media violence and gun control to that of behavioral health. Her son, she later learns, was not just merely on a murder hunt; he was on a suicide mission.

That nuanced untangling of a complex knot of issues set Klebold on a new mission of teaching others how to recognize the signs of suicidal ideation. Ones that she – and many others — sadly missed. One of the more poignant moments I felt from her article was when she described her difficulties re-entering the world after her son, whom she loved, stained it with unspeakable terror. Klebold recounts moments of inexplicable emotional undoing caused by her overwhelming suffering, like the time she wept inconsolably at the sight of a dead pigeon in a parking lot.

While of course I realize that our stories are vastly different, in thinking back on this article, I can identify with the pain Klebold was carrying. Trauma can make us do crazy, irrational things. At times, we do not understand or recognize ourselves, much less our behaviors or reactions to otherwise mundane things. You feel confused, misunderstood and, at times, altogether lost. But with patient, supported and intense self-reflection, we can begin to make sense of trauma's aftershocks. Learning how to prepare for and stabilize in triggering moments takes hard work (and, I believe, professional help), but if you choose to see these patterns as lessons along a healing path, it is possible to move forward and toward rediscovering yourself.

In the time shortly after my cancer treatment when I was reentering "the wild," as I called it, I felt obligated to adopt a new post-cancer persona. I was no longer protected by the bubble of treatment and my safety net of supporters. At first, I tried to use humor as an icebreaker for those I hadn't seen since my diagnosis and treatment. In one instance, I was greeted warmly by a colleague who was seeing me for the first time since I returned from my medical leave.

"You look…pretty—pretty good," he stammered and patted me on the shoulder.

I sensed he was searched to be polite while also registering how I *really* looked—hair missing in patches, twenty-plus pounds packed on from meds and pregnancy, and my right eye misshapen from the tumor.

"Pretty good?" I scoffed. "I guess that's better than, 'Hey, you're not dead yet!'"

We both laughed, him more genuinely than me. It got us past that uncomfortable initial greeting, but I knew it didn't feel right.

On another, similar occasion, a coworker told me, "It's so great to see you!"

"Well, you know what they say," I offered, "better to be seen than to be viewed!"

Again, we both laughed—he more so than I.

The humor angle wouldn't work, I soon realized. Maybe it did for others, but not for me. I felt as though I was betraying myself by making a joke out of my most painful life event. I decided, after that last interaction, I would no longer worry about lightening the mood or softening the ground for others at my expense. I owed it to myself and, to this day, I still honor that debt.

People often wonder about the right thing to say to someone with cancer. On some days, I would get offended if someone didn't ask about my health; other times, I would get offended when they did. It simply depended on the gauge in my emotional support gas tank, which swung like a pendulum between empty and full in those early days of remission.

I've come to learn others' perceptions or reactions to me was really none of my business. I have no way of controlling or knowing how their own journeys with cancer or other chronic diseases would shape their interactions with me. It took me a long time to realize when some seemed uncomfortable or standoffish with me, it really wasn't about *me*. It had more to do with the collective experiences and associations with disease they were bringing to the interaction. Perhaps it scared or saddened them. It may have rekindled a memory of a loved one's suffering even from as far back as childhood. Either way, I learned over the years cancer *is* a loaded word and, out of respect for others and myself, I temper how and with whom I share the term.

This was another struggle I felt with remission: when and with whom I should share my story. How would I bring this up to new people in my life? Would I talk about it at all? Or mention it too soon? Or too late?

Of the two, there were probably more times when I would disclose my brain tumor immediately and felt the awkward space between my "confession" and its absorption to the person with whom I was speaking. For example, a few months after my diagnosis, my daughter had a daycare friend over for a Saturday afternoon playdate. I knew the child's mother from coming and goings at the daycare center, exchanging polite conversation as we passed one another. I didn't know her well enough to say we were genuinely friends, however. When she brought her son over to play, she had a few errands to run while he stayed for Play-Doh and games with my daughter. I pulled her aside before she left and stunned her with, "Just so you know, I just found out that I have a brain tumor." I went on to explain I wanted her to know in case my daughter mentioned anything to her son about it (to be clear, we heeded the oncologist's advice and waited years before gently telling my daughter, in an age-appropriate way, about my brain tumor—doing so sooner would have been too difficult for her to understand). Instead of using words like "tumor" or "cancer," we simply said I was sick and needed special medicine to get better. Funny thing about kids—they're very literal. I found that keeping my situation in the simplest terms satisfied my child's need to understand while not burdening her with worry. Still, I was concerned she may have heard the term "brain tumor" or absorbed it in the tense air of our home like toddler osmosis.

The child's mom offered the usual "I'm-so-sorry" sympathies but the concern in her face seemed less about me and more about the safety of her son, as if she were asking herself, *Should I really leave him here? Maybe I should stay? Is this woman crazy? Is she sick?* and so on. I reassured her I was feeling fine and it wouldn't affect their playdate in any way, to which she politely agreed and went on to run her errands. The playdate did go on without incident and without any mention of a brain tumor by my daughter to her son.

Looking back now, I wonder now how that news affected that mom's day. How many people did she go on to discuss our interaction? What triggers did it release in her or others? How did it shape her impressions of me? Of my family? Of what a brain tumor "looks like"?

To this day, I don't know the answer to any of those questions. I do know this was the first of many times in which I would blurt out my cancer in ways that seemed appropriate to me at the time but, with the benefit of hindsight, were hardly necessary. I suppose there were times when I felt obligated to let anyone and everyone know I was carrying this "secret" and I felt compelled to unburden myself. By doing so, I realize now I was selfishly burdening others. I wish I'd known that sooner.

For a while, I told neighbors, co-workers, and strangers I'd just met in the street. I continued this pattern until I thought less about myself and more about others, especially my immediate family. How would it feel to my children to have someone, even with the best of intentions, ask about their mother's cancer? It was bad enough I was receiving solicitations in the mail on local available gravesites; did I really want my husband to be stopped in the grocery store from concerned teachers or other parents hanging out on the town's gossip grapevine?

And so, I went on to adopt a more reserved and private approach to sharing my cancer with others. Only if I felt safe and entrusted with the individual would I share the gift of my story. And that's how I came to see it—as a gift to myself and to the world about the miracle of healing and overcoming a mountain of odds stacked so steep and so sharply I could not help but marvel that I safely hiked its terrain.

More than a pardon or forgiveness, I began to settle into remission as an opportunity, not a threat. By changing my attitude toward my circumstance, I know for sure I was able to change my life. I gave at any and every opportunity. I started saying "yes" instead of "no" to new adventures and connections. I reminded myself about the possibilities that come with an unknown future.

No longer reeling in the awkward and bitter state of remission, I was poised to chart a new course. I was not just in remission; I was now on a *re-mission*. That subtle, but profound shift in my thinking is what got me through the storm and to the rainbow.

"Hope is really a thought process made up of …

a trilogy of goals, pathways, and agency."

– Brené Brown

As Brené Brown shares in the quote above and her book *Atlas of the Heart*, hope is a choice we make in the moments of life's friction, not peace. It arrives when we identify our goals and pathways while believing wholeheartedly in our ability to achieve both. Here is my interpretation of how you can develop goals, pathways and agency that Brown describes:

Goals: What can you do that will add joy to your life? Think of an experience you absolutely cannot wait to do again. Write it down and make it happen.

Pathways: Set out for your goals, be ready for change and adjust your footing along the way with the knowledge that the bigger the storm, the brighter the rainbow.

Agency: Believe in yourself. Remember your past struggles (we've all had them) and how you persevered. In times of doubt, say, "This is all going to be fine." Decide that it cannot be anything else but that.

"Say 'Thank You' because your faith is so strong that you don't doubt that whatever the problem, you'll get through it. You're saying thank you because you know that even in the eye of the storm, God has put a rainbow in the clouds."

— Oprah Winfrey

Chapter 7

The Rainbow

Six years after treatment, I headed to Nashville, Tennessee to meet up with my lifelong best friend for a long weekend of dancing, revelry, and celebration in honor of my fortieth birthday. Decked out in red-bottomed Christian Louboutin high heels and a princess birthday crown with matching sash, I was thrilled to fully indulge in this magnificent town. Birthdays after cancer are especially sacred and I was thrilled to become, not just turn, into another decade of life.

It was my second visit to the bright lights and big music city; I attended a conference a year prior and fell in love with its charm, charisma, and electrifying energy. "If my soul were a city," I remember telling my best friend, "*this* would be it."

Nashville is a place where everyone is welcome—country music fans, rock and rollers, and romantics alike are drawn by its magnetism. The incredible musical talent on display at seemingly endless venues stretched out along Broadway Street—the heart of its downtown nightlife—pulsates so fervently I felt like I was vibrating, not just walking, through the city. Perhaps it's because I've always been a lover of all music genres or maybe it was the glow of strangers buzzing with excitement, tearing loose from their daily grinds, but something about Nashville awoke *something* in me.

In the second half of life, these "Nashville moments," as I call them, continue to surprise and delight me. Without realizing it, I started to let go of the fear and embrace new opportunities for myself. I quit working in healthcare and took a job in higher education, an industry that shared my passion for learning, reaching back to my academia roots. This new opportunity introduced new friendships and connections. I let go of old relationships that no longer worked or totally fulfilled me. I started running to stay active—first a mile, then three miles and, before I knew it, I was running up mountains—literally—ascending more than 400 feet of elevation at a clip.

The first time I tackled a mountain on a run, I was hooked.

Up there, I wasn't a wife or a mother, a daughter, a sister, or sister-in-law. No one and nothing, not even the ghost of cancer, could reach me there. I felt freer than I had my whole life. (No wonder so many fairy tales begin with, "In a land far, far away.") Emotionally untethered and carried by the breeze, I gulped down the scents of honeysuckle and lilac in the air. I delighted in the chirps, coos, and whistles of the birds. I felt—for the first time in a long time—as though I had cleared, quite literally, a mountain of anxiety and worry. The quiet space during my runs gave me a chance to meditate on my true purpose in this life. By getting quiet, I was able to hear the whisper that was speaking to me for years: tell your story. Speak your truth. Share your journey.

And that is what brought me here. Although the passing years have been bittersweet, I recognize my journey has been stretched far beyond the anticipated expiration date. I have enjoyed an extraordinary gift denied by many: the blessing of more time. More time to reflect, learn and grow. For that, I'm deeply grateful. To this day, we don't know how much longer I have. We aren't any closer to understanding the nature of my glitch than we were on December 26, 2014. Still, we go on with the gratitude for the time I've had and the value of its meaning. I hope my lessons learned from this extraordinary gift can offer you a little lift along the climb, wherever it's taking you.

There have been times when I've asked myself, *Did the cancer ruin my life?* Earlier in my journey, I would have answered with a resounding *yes*. Now, with the benefit and grace of time, I can say the cancer changed, but did not ruin my life.

Without knowing my story, one would never suspect that I have a cancerous tumor at the hub of my body's core functioning unit. Nor would they suspect that I underwent brain surgery, radiation treatment and vision therapy. Living with an invisible illness taught me compassion and, while there are surely times I slip up, I more often view the world as though everyone is carrying some measure of pain. And whether that's a diagnosis of cancer, the loss of a loved one or a bout of self-doubt, the root of that suffering is irrelevant because all pain essentially feels the same. Whether we feel shamed, robbed or unworthy, we all carry the weight of something brewing beneath the surface. When we recognize that, we begin to see people, and perhaps ourselves, differently – a bit more gently and with more compassion.

Cancer slowed me down and lifted my head from the everyday chaos of life – the deadlines, full inboxes, petty arguments, toddler struggles, endless checklists, dirty diapers, events calendars, body image insecurities – all of it. It forced me to retrace my steps and examine, then re-examine, my journey while honoring, but not lingering long enough to regret, the past. Taking stock of my life provided me with immense comfort; it reminded me of the hurdles I'd previously cleared – and how. It showed me that, while my cancer diagnosis will always be a significant chapter in my life, it is not and will not be my whole story. I realized that, while I've changed, I am effectively still the same person as the little girl who frolicked outside, the feisty teen who debated her hungry heart out, the awkward college-then-graduate student who pushed past imposter syndrome, and the wife turned mother raising humans who themselves could go on to become professionals, spouses, parents and, yes, even patients. Perhaps they, too, can make their way with a little help from a peek into the other side of their mother's cancer journey. The messy, imperfect, unexpected storm of survival then re-mission.

Walking in the patient's shoes and finding that realities were, at times, disjointed from the promises healthcare brands were projecting to their prospective patients (myself guilty of doing this while I worked in healthcare marketing) further underscored the high and low moments of my "Year of the Patient." Sharing these lessons with others emboldened a sense of real purpose that could be harnessed from my experience. I offer these up to friends, neighbors, and colleagues when, and as gently, as I can. Knowing that everyone's healthcare journey is different, I'm careful to caveat these experiences as unique to my patient story while also emphasizing that everything matters in the delivery of healthcare. If the provider does not look you in the eye before they look at your chart; if the nurse does not introduce themselves at change of shift; if the registration staff seems inconvenienced by your needs; if the invoices are confusing or incorrect – every bit of it matters in how it feels to the patient and their loved ones. Working in healthcare is exceptionally difficult, I understand. However, if systems are making claims about being "patient-centered" or "world class," it must be pulled through the entire process. If it isn't, the patient trust can be irreparably broken, and all the other efforts of the team are essentially discarded as the patient eventually moves on to another brand that gets it right. Although not everyone has the luxury of comparison shopping in healthcare today (insurance coverage, limited access in rural communities, a provider who is so excellent that patients tolerate the kinks, etc.), I suspect that by the time my children are adult patients, it will become easier as market disrupters grasp an even firmer hold on the business, forcing health systems to compete and perform with excellence at every turn.

Allowing quiet reflection to reset mid-road enabled me to face, then release the ghosts of remission by accepting a new, more open outlook on my future. With help and a newfound passion for running, I wrestled down depression and anxiety, cancer's two favorite children. I could then see the rays of hope life was sending me during the storm. I felt this as I chose to accept my unknown prognosis as an invitation, not impediment, to the future. I saw this as I watched my son learn to crawl then walk, heard my daughter attempt then master the flute, discovered the thrill of a new favorite city, and changed careers for one that challenged but did not exhaust me. The knowledge that we all long to connect on a journey with an undetermined ending emboldened the re-mission of sharing my story for whatever it is worth: hope, humor, or advocacy from experiencing healthcare on the frontlines.

Lastly, and perhaps most importantly of all, cancer locked in the great lesson that we're all told, but we don't quite seem to catch until everything hangs in the balance: that the only moment we truly own is the present. Finally learning this allowed me to live boldly, bravely, and more mindfully, while savoring simple pleasures more deeply. The rush of juice from a fresh garden tomato or perfectly ripe peach. When the wind finally hooks a kite and it rocks gently, marvelously in the sky. The joy of sipping a bold, strong cup of coffee each morning. Catching the breeze on my back during a steamy, hot summer run. Laughing to the point of tears with some of my oldest and dearest friends. Holding my son's hand on a walk, still. Seeing my daughter intuitively choose kindness over judgment during simple, everyday conversation. Relishing an old familiar song and the thrill of discovering new favorites again and again. These are not life's most precious moments, but strung together, they are the essential fabric of a meaningful existence. I am sure I would have overlooked their magnificence had I not been in a position to imagine losing them altogether. In the end, I believe that facing my mortality taught me the art of living more fully.

And perhaps that's the best we can all do to survive anything that is thrown at us as we make our way, finding the whole in the balance of all life's dichotomies – suffering while surviving, hurting through growth, grieving while living still. Storms that clear our path to forge new rainbows. On my best days, I like to view the ironic life lessons gleaned from my cancer story and my unexpected survival in the same way that my journey began: to be hoisted in the air and declared, "Is this not the most beautiful thing you have ever seen?"

While I believe my story is unique, I know it is far from original. At some point, everyone is shown that life can change in a matter of seconds. In fact, by the time you finish reading this sentence, someone somewhere will receive ground-shifting news. Whether that's a devastating diagnosis, a shocking confession, an untimely death, or the loss of a precious piece of identity, life altering events are always happening all around us, all the time. But here's the good news: in the end, it's not the life-altering event that defines who you are. Rather, it's your response to the event that measures one's character. It's what mines the heart for the truest expression of who you really are. It's the most definitive way—the *only* way, in fact—of showing one's resilience to the kind of adversity that tests the grit of the soul.

As the great Grantland Rice so eloquently stated, "For when the One Great Scorer comes to mark against your name, He writes not that you won or lost, but how you played the game." I too believe how you recover from a personal storm is far more important than the debris and destruction it left behind.

For sure, my life will not be defined by the storm but by all that happened after—the moments of pain that yielded growth and new opportunity, all leading up to my greatest calling and my best life possible.

As I write this, I recall last weekend my husband and I planted a new hydrangea plant in our yard. Believe it or not, there was a time when I could not fathom the idea of doing that—it would be too painful, too sad for me. It was a period of time in my life when I stopped planting seeds, both literally and proverbially. I would be anguished by the idea of not being here to see the blossom.

It's amazing how a thought that used to cause an emotional unraveling no longer even phases me; in fact, it hadn't even crossed my mind. Instead, I was delighted to think of the bountiful bouquets this plant would yield for our kitchen table and those of our friends and neighbors.

No longer in a place of reeling but in a position of having climbed the mountains and looking ahead at the terrain with new vision, a colorful arc of possibility is now clear. I'm experiencing the second act I never saw coming. A new career, a new decade and a new world of opportunities awaits.

And that's how my rainbow, like all rainbows, emerged: as a magical, wondrous phenomenon produced by reflection and the sun shining through the rain. Wherever you are on your life's journey, I hope you too can find a way to weather the storm, conquer the mountain, and find hope in the form of new relationships, exciting possibilities and more adventures. Whether through time, lessons learned, the love of others, or the reflection within yourself, I sincerely hope you find a way to your rainbow.

And, once you find it, picture me on the other side, whispering to you, "Yes, I've got it too. And now that we have it, may we never let it go."

"'Hope' is the thing with feathers -

That perches in the soul -

And sings the tune without the words -

And never stops - at all -

And sweetest - in the Gale - is heard -

And sore must be the storm -

That could abash the little Bird

That kept so many warm -

I've heard it in the chillest land -

And on the strangest Sea -

Yet - never - in Extremity,

It asked a crumb - of me."
            - Emily Dickinson